Me and My Friends

I Can
Listen

written by Daniel Nunn

illustrated by Clare Elsom

raintree

Raintree is an imprint of Capstone Global Library Limited,
a company incorporated in England and Wales having
its registered office at 7 Pilgrim Street, London, EC4V 6LB –
Registered company number: 6695582

www.raintreepublishers.co.uk
myorders@raintreepublishers.co.uk

Edited by Brynn Baker
Designed by Steve Mead and Kyle Grenz
Production by Helen McCreath
Original illustrations © Clare Elsom
Originated by Capstone Global Library Ltd
Printed and bound in China by LEO

ISBN 978 1 406 28162 0 (hardback)
18 17 16 15 14
10 9 8 7 6 5 4 3 2 1

ISBN 978 1 406 28167 5 (paperback)
19 18 17 16 15
10 9 8 7 6 5 4 3 2

British Library Cataloguing in Publication Data
A full catalogue record for this book is available from the
British Library.

Contents

Listening

I listen to my friend.

My friend listens to me.

I listen to my mum.

My mum listens to me.

I listen to my brother.

My brother listens to me.

I listen to my sister.

My sister listens to me.

I listen to my dad.

My dad listens to me.

I listen to my teacher.

My teacher listens to me.

I listen to our dog.

Our dog listens to me.

I listen to everyone!

Everyone listens to me!

Listening quiz

Which of these pictures
shows listening?

Did listening make this child happy? Why? Do you listen?

Picture glossary

friend person you care about and have fun with

listen to hear with your ears, paying close attention to what someone is saying

Index

Notes for teachers and parents

BEFORE READING

Building background: Ask children who they listen to during the school day. (Friends, teachers, bus drivers.) To whom do they talk when they get home? (Family members.)

AFTER READING

Recall and reflection: Ask children to look at page 13. Ask them what the girl and her dad are talking about. Ask children to look at page 9. Ask what the brothers are talking about.

Sentence knowledge: Ask children to find a capital letter and a full stop in the book. Why is there a capital letter? Why is there a full stop?

Word knowledge (phonics): Ask children to point to the word *dad* on page 12. Sound out the three phonemes in the word *d/a/d*. Ask children to sound out each phoneme as they point at the letters, and then blend the sounds together to make the word *dad*. Ask children to name some words that rhyme with *dad*. (Glad, sad, mad, bad.)

Word recognition: Ask children to count how many times the word *listen/listens* appears in the main text (not counting the quiz). (16)

AFTER-READING ACTIVITIES

Ask children to work with partners to listen and speak. As one child tells about a topic, such as what he or she did over the weekend, the other should listen and then name two things he or she remembers from listening. Then the partners should switch roles.

In this book

Topic
listening

Topic words
brother
dad
everyone
friend
listen
mum
sister
teacher

Sentence stems
I ___ to my mum.
Our ___ ___ to me.
I ___ to my ___.
My ___ listens to ___.

High-frequency words
I
our
me
my
to